Animal Jokes

Say...what kind of dog tells time?

A WATCH DOG!

TICK
TICK
TICK
TICK

with **Glen Singleton**

Crazy Book of Animal Jokes
First published in 2003 by Hinkler Books Pty Ltd
17–23 Redwood Drive
Dingley VIC 3172 Australia
www.hinklerbooks.com

© Hinkler Books Pty Ltd 2003
Reprinted 2003

ISBN: 1865156884

Cover designer: Peter Tovey Studios
Editor: Rose Inserra
Typesetting: Midland Typesetters
Printed and bound in Australia

Crazy Book of Animal Jokes

Why are four-legged animals bad dancers?

Because they have two left feet.

Are you a vegetarian because
you love animals?

No, because I don't like plants.

What has an elephant's trunk,
a tiger's stripes, a giraffe's neck
and a baboon's bottom?

A zoo.

What does an echidna have for lunch?

Prickled onions.

Why should you never fight an echidna?

Because it will always win on points.

Why do mother kangaroos hate rainy days?

Because their kids have to play inside.

Why don't kangaroos ride bicycles?

*Because they don't have thumbs to
ring the little bell.*

When do kangaroos celebrate their
birthdays?

During leap year.

What is big and grey and out of bounds?

A tired kangaroo.

Why was the kangaroo mad at her children?

Because they were jumping on the bed.

Why did the koala fall out of the tree?

Because it was dead.

4

Why did the bat miss the train?

Because it spent too long hanging around.

Why do bears have fur coats?

Because they can't get plastic raincoats in their size!

A grizzly bear walks into a bar and says to the bartender, 'I'll have a gin........................and tonic.'

Bartender: 'What's with the big pause?'

Bear: 'I don't know. My father had them too.'

Why was the little bear spoilt?

Because he was panda'd to.

What's big white and furry and found
in outback Australia?

A very lost polar bear.

Which song do beavers sing?

'Gnawing me, gnawing you.'

What did the beaver say to the tree?

It's been nice gnawing you.

Where do bees go when they're sick?

To the waspital!

What kinds of bees fight?

Rumble Bees!

What are a bee's favourite soap operas?

*The Bold & The Bee-utiful
and Days of our Hives!*

Why was the bee's hair sticky?

Because he used a honey-comb!

What did one bee say to her
nosy neighbour bee?

'Mind your own bees' nest!'

What happened to the male
bee that fell in love?

He got stuck on his honey.

How do bees travel?

They take the buzz!

'**A** bee just stung me on the arm.'

'Which one?'

'I don't know. They all look alike to me.'

What did the teacher say
to the naughty bee?

'Bee-hive yourself.'

What do bees do with their honey?

They cell it.

What do you call a bee that buzzes quietly?

A mumble bee.

What is a bee's favourite meal?

A humburger.

What's the healthiest insect?

A Vitamin Bee.

What do bees wear to work?

Buzzness suits.

Where did Noah keep the bees?

In the ark hives.

What do bees use to communicate
with each other?

Their cell phone.

What do you call a woodpecker
with no beak?

A headbanger.

Which bird can never be trusted?

A lyre-bird.

Which bird can lift the heaviest weights?

A crane.

Which bird succeeds?

A budgie without teeth.

What's the definition of illegal?

A sick bird.

Did you hear about the performer who specialised in bird impressions?

He ate worms.

Which bird tastes just like butter?

A stork.

Which type of bird steals from banks?

A robin.

What do you call a bird that
lives underground?

A mynah bird.

What is a crowbar?

A place were crows go to get a drink!

Which bird is always out of breath?

A puffin.

Which language do birds speak?

Pigeon English.

What do you give a sick bird?

Tweetment.

Why does a hummingbird hum?

It doesn't know the words!

Why do birds fly south?

It's too far to walk!

What are feathers good for?

Birds.

Why is the sky so high?

So birds won't bump their heads.

Why don't baby birds smile?

*Would you smile if your mother
fed you worms all day?*

What's the difference between
a bird and a fly?

A bird can fly but a fly can't bird.

What's black and white and very noisy?

A magpie with a drum kit.

What's bright orange and
sounds like a parrot?

A carrot!

Why did the parrot wear a raincoat?

Because it wanted to be polly unsaturated.

What did the canary say when
she laid a square egg?

'Ouch!'

What's a pelican's favourite dish?

Anything that fits the bill.

What did the goose say when he got cold?

'I have people-bumps!'

What did the parrot say when it fell
in love with the frog?

'Polly wants a croaker!'

What do you get when you run a sparrow
over with a lawn mower?

Shredded tweet.

What is a polygon?

A dead parrot.

Why did the owl 'owl?

Because the woodpecker would peck 'er.

What do owls sing when it's raining?

'Too wet to woo.'

How do we know that owls are smarter than chickens?

Have you ever heard of Kentucky-fried owl?

What does an educated owl say?

'Whom.'

What happened when the owl lost his voice?

He didn't give a hoot.

What's got six legs and can fly long distances?

Three swallows.

What do vultures always have for dinner?

Leftovers.

What flies through the jungle
singing operetta?

The parrots of Penzance.

What do baby swans dance to?

Cygnet-ure tunes.

What did the little bird say to the big bird?

'Peck on someone your own size.'

What is a parrot's favourite game?

Hide and Speak.

What do you call a Scottish parrot?

A Macaw.

How do hens dance?

Chick to chick.

What did the 100 kilo parrot say?

'Polly want a cracker, NOW!'

What do you call a well-behaved goose?

A propaganda.

When is the best time to buy a canary?

When it is going cheap.

What do parrots eat?

Polyfilla.

Why does a stork stand on one leg?

Because it would fall over if it
lifted the other one.

Why do buffaloes always travel in herds?

Because they're afraid of getting
mugged by elephants.

What did the mother buffalo say to her son
when he left for school?

'Bison.'

What's the difference between
a buffalo and a bison?

You can't wash your hands in a buffalo.

What did the caterpillar say to the butterfly?

You'll never get me up in one of those things.

Why wasn't the butterfly invited
to the dance?

Because it was a moth ball.

What does a caterpillar do on
New Year's Day?

Turns over a new leaf.

What do you call an unmarried female moth?

Myth.

What's the biggest moth in the world?

A mam-moth.

What flies around your light at night
and can bite off your head?

A tiger moth.

What do you call a camel with three humps?

Humphrey.

What do you call a camel with no humps?

A horse.

If horses wear shoes what do camels wear?

Desert boots.

Why don't cats shave?

Because they prefer Whiskas.

Why did the cat put the letter 'M' into the freezer?

Because it turns 'ice' into 'mice'.

What type of cats go bowling?

Alley cats.

Now you see it, now you don't, now you see it, now you don't. What is it?

A black cat on a zebra crossing.

ONE OF THOSE DANGEROUS BLACK SPACES BETWEEN THE WHITE ONES ➞

Where do cats go for a school excursion?

The mewseum.

What looks like half a cat?

The other half.

What kind of cat loves swimming?

An octopussy.

What has four legs and flies?

A dead cat.

What do you call a cat who loses a fight?

Claude.

What happened to the cat that
swallowed a ball of wool?

She had mittens.

What do you call a cat that
lives in a hospital?

A first aid kit.

What do you call a Chinese cat that
spies through windows?

A Peking tom.

What do cats eat as a special treat?

Mice creams.

Ten cats were on a boat, one jumped off,
how many were left?

None, they were all copycats!

What did the cat say when
it lost all its money?

'I'm paw.'

What did the cat have for breakfast?

Mice bubbles.

What kind of cat shouldn't
you play cards with?

A cheetah!

'Did you put the cat out?'

'I didn't know it was on fire!'

What do you call a messy cat?

Kitty litter.

What goes '99 bonk'?

A centipede with a wooden leg.

What lies down 100 feet in the air?

A centipede.

What has 75 pairs of sneakers, a ball and two hoops?

A centipede basketball team.

Why was the father centipede so upset?

All of the kids needed new shoes!

Why did the insects drop the centipede
from their football team?

He took too long to put on his boots!

Which side of the chicken has
the most feathers?

The outside.

Why did the chicken cross the road?

To see the man laying bricks.

Why did the goose cross the road?

To prove it wasn't chicken.

Why did the chicken cross the road, roll in the mud and cross the road again?

Because he was a dirty double-crosser.

Why was the chicken sick?

Because it had people pox.

What is white, lives in the Himalayas and lays eggs?

The Abominable Snow Chicken.

What do you call a crazy chicken?

A cuckoo cluck.

What do you call a chicken that
lays lightbulbs?

A battery hen.

Did you hear about the naughty chicken?

It was eggspelled from school.

What do you call the ghost of a chicken?

A poultrygeist.

Where do chickens go to die?

To oven.

Why did the chicken join the band?

Because it had drumsticks.

Why did the rooster refuse to fight?

Because he was chicken.

Why don't turkeys get invited
to dinner parties?

Because they use fowl language.

Why do chickens watch TV?

For hentertainment.

Who is the most feared animal of all?

Attila the hen.

What did Mr. and Mrs. Chicken
call their baby?

Egg.

Which hen lays the longest?

A dead one.

Why did the man cross a
chicken with an octopus?

*So everyone in his family could
have a leg each.*

What do you get when you sit under a cow?

A pat on the head.

What do you get from nervous cows?

Milk shakes.

What happened when the cow jumped over the barbed wire fence?

It was an udder catastrophe!

Why did the cow jump over the moon?

Because the farmer had cold hands.

What did the astronauts say when
they found bones on the moon?

The cow didn't make it!

What has four legs and goes 'Boo'?

A cow with a cold.

Why do cows wear bells?

Because their horns don't work!

What goes 'oom, oom'?

A cow walking backwards.

What do cows eat for breakfast?

Mooslie.

Cow 1: 'Are you concerned about catching mad cow disease?'

Cow 2: 'Not at all. I'm a sheep.'

How do cows count?

They use a cowculator.

What did the bull say to the cow?

'I'll love you for heifer and heifer.'

What do cows listen to?

Moosic.

What do you call a cow that eats grass?

A lawn mooer.

What do you call a cow that lives
at the North Pole?

An eskimoo.

What do you call cattle that always sit down?

Ground beef.

What do frozen cows do?

They give ice cream.

What game do cows play at parties?

Moosical chairs.

What is a cow's favourite film?

'The Sound of Moosic.'

What is a cow's favourite singer?

Moodonna.

Where did the cow go for its holiday?

Moo Zealand.

Where do cows go for entertainment?

The Moovies.

Which TV show do cows never miss?

The moos.

What would you do if a bull charged you?

Pay him cash.

What steps would you take
if a bull chased you?

Big ones.

What do you call a sleeping bull?

A bulldozer!

What is a crocodile's favourite game?

Snap.

What time is it when you see a crocodile?

Time to run.

Why was the crocodile called Kodak?

Because it was always snapping.

Who was the first deer astronaut?

Buck Rogers.

What do you call a deer with only one eye?

No idea.

What do you call a deer with
no legs and only one eye?

Still no idea.

What animal drops from the clouds?

A raindeer.

What did the dog say when he
was attacked by a tiger?

Nothing, dogs can't talk.

Why is a dog's nose in the middle of its face?

Because it's the scenter.

What do dogs and trees have in common?

Bark!

What do you say to a dog before he eats?

'Bone appetit!'

Why are dogs like hamburgers?

They're both sold by the pound.

What do you give a dog with a fever?

Mustard, it's the best thing for a hot dog!

What do you call a group
of boring, spotted dogs?

101 Dull-matians!

What kind of dog tells time?

A watch dog!

Where do you put a noisy dog?

In a barking lot!

What's the difference between a
well dressed man and a tired dog?

The man wears a suit, the dog just pants.

Why does a dog wag its tail?

Because no one else will do it for him.

What did the dog say when
he sat on the sandpaper?

'Rough, rough!'

What is more fantastic than a talking dog?

A spelling bee!

'**D**oes your dog bite?'

'No.'

'Oww. I thought you said
your dog doesn't bite.'

'That's not my dog.'

Customer: 'Have you got any
dogs going cheap?'

*Pet Shop Owner: 'No, I'm afraid
they all go woof.'*

Did you hear the one about the dog running ten kilometres to retrieve a stick?

It was too far-fetched.

'I play Scrabble with my pet dog every night.'

'He must be clever.'

'I don't know about that. I usually beat him.'

'I've lost my dog.'

'Put an ad in the paper.'

'Don't be silly. He can't read.'

How do you know when
it's raining cats and dogs?

You step into a poodle.

How do you stop a dog doing
his business in the hall?

Put him outside.

When is a brown dog not a brown dog?

When it is a greyhound.

Where would you find a dog with no legs?

Exactly where you left it.

What happened to the dog that swallowed the watch?

He got ticks.

Why did the dog cross the street?

To slobber on the other side.

What's the difference between a
barking dog and an umbrella?

You can shut the umbrella up.

What do ducks watch on TV?

Duckumentaries.

What kind of doctor treats ducks?

A quack.

Did you hear about the duck decorator?

He papered over the quacks.

Customer: 'How much for the duck?'

Pet shop owner: '$20.'

Customer: 'I only have $15.
Can you send me the bill?'

*Pet shop owner: 'No, you'll have
to take the whole duck.'*

What's another name for a clever duck?

A wise quacker!

What happens when ducks fly upside-down?

They quack up.

Why did the duck go ring-ring?

He got a phone bill.

Which birds steal the soap from the bath?

Robber ducks.

What's the difference between a gym
instructor and a duck?

*One goes quick on its legs and the
other goes quack on its legs!*

How do ducks play tennis?

With a quacket.

What is a duck's favourite TV show?

The feather forecast.

What do you call a crate of ducks?

A box of quackers.

What did the duck say to the comedian after the show?

'You really quacked me up!'

What do you call a duck with fangs?

Count Quackula.

What do you get when you cross
an elephant with a fish?

Swimming trunks!

What do you get when an elephant
sits on your friend?

A flat mate.

What do you call an elephant
in a telephone box?

Stuck.

hat do you call an elephant
that never washes?

A smellyphant.

How do you get six elephants
in a fire engine?

*Two in the front, two in the back and two on
top going 'Eeeeawww, eeeeawww'.*

What do you give a sick elephant?

A very big paper bag.

Why do elephants live in the jungle?

Because they can't fit inside houses.

Why are elephants wrinkled all over?

Because they can't fit on an ironing board.

What's the difference between
an elephant and a flea?

*An elephant can have fleas but a
flea can't have elephants.*

What time is it when an elephant
sits on your fence?

Time to get a new fence.

What did Thomas Edison Elephant invent?

The electric peanut.

'Have you ever found an elephant
in your custard?'

'No.'

'It must work then!'

Why did the elephant paint the
bottom of his feet yellow?

So he could hide upside down in custard

What did Tarzan say when he saw the
elephants coming over the hill?

Here come the elephants over the hill.

What do a grape and an elephant
have in common?

They're both purple, except for the elephant!

How do you fit an elephant into a matchbox?

Take out the matches!

How do you fit a tiger into a matchbox?

Take out the elephant!

'**D**id you know that elephants never forget?'

'*What do they have to remember?*'

Why is a snail stronger than an elephant?

A snail carries its house, and an elephant only carries his trunk!

Why is an elephant large, grey and wrinkled?

Because if it was small, white and smooth it would be an aspirin!

How can you tell an elephant from a banana?

Try to lift it up. If you can't, it's either an elephant or a very heavy banana.

What game do elephants play in a Volkswagen?

Squash!

How does an elephant get down from a tree?

He sits on a leaf and waits for autumn.

Why do elephants' tusks stick out?

Because their parents can't afford braces!

Where can you buy ancient elephants?

At a mammoth sale.

How do you stop an elephant from smelling?

Tie a knot in his trunk.

What's bright blue and very heavy?

An elephant holding its breath.

What's the same size and shape as an
elephant but weighs nothing?

An elephant's shadow.

How do you get an elephant
up an acorn tree?

Sit him on an acorn and wait twenty years.

Why are elephants grey?

So you can tell them apart from canaries.

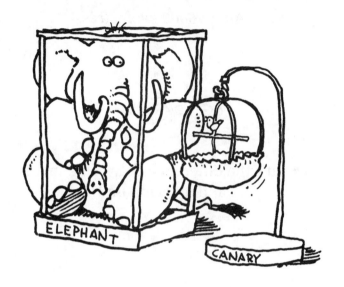

How do you get down from an elephant?

*You don't get down from an elephant,
you get down from a duck.*

What do elephants have that
no other animal does?

Baby elephants.

What's the difference between an African
elephant and an Indian elephant?

About 6000 kilometres.

What's the difference between a mouse
and an elephant?

About a ton.

Why do elephants never get rich?

Because they work for peanuts.

What time is it when an elephant
climbs into your bed?

Time to get a new bed.

What do elephants take when
they can't sleep?

Trunkquilisers.

Which animals were the last to leave the ark?

*The elephants – they were
packing their trunks.*

'**M**y dad is so short-sighted that he can't get to sleep unless he counts elephants!'

How do you get an elephant into a car?

Open the door.

How does the elephant get out of the car?

The same way it got in.

How do you know when there is
an elephant in the oven?

You can't close the door.

How do you know when an elephant
has been using your phone?

You've been charged for trunk calls.

How do you know peanuts are fattening?

Have you ever seen a skinny elephant?

How do you know when there is
an elephant in the fridge?

There are footprints in the butter.

Why can't an elephant ride a tricycle?

*Because it doesn't have thumbs
to ring the bell!*

What did the mouse say to the elephant?

Squeak.

Did you hear about the elephant
that drank a bottle of rum?

He got trunk.

Why do elephants have wrinkled knees?

From playing marbles.

What do you call an elephant that
flies straight up?

An elecopter.

What do you call an elephant that flies?

A jumbo jet.

What do you call the red stuff between an elephant's toes?

A slow hunter.

What do you give an elephant with diarrhoea?

Plenty of room.

Why do elephants have wrinkles
on their skin?

Because they've stayed in the bath too long.

What is big, grey and wears glass slippers?

Cinderelephant.

What is grey with sixteen wheels?

An elephant on roller-skates!

Where do elephants go on holidays?

Tuscany.

Why do elephants have Big Ears?

Because Noddy wouldn't pay the ransom.

Why do elephants have trunks?

*Because they can't fit everything
into a handbag.*

Why do elephants wear sneakers?

So they can sneak up on mice.

Why was the elephant standing
on the marshmallow?

He didn't want to fall in the hot chocolate.

Where do baby elephants come from?

Very big storks.

Why did the zookeeper refuse to work in the elephant enclosure?

Because the work kept piling up.

What is big, green and has a trunk?

An unripe elephant.

How do goldfish go into business?

They start on a small scale.

What is an octopus's favourite song?

'I want to hold your hand, hand, hand, hand, I want to hold your hand, hand, hand, hand.'

What does an octopus wear when it's cold?

A coat of arms.

What do you call a neurotic octopus?

A crazy, mixed-up squid.

What's the difference between
a piano and a fish?

You can tune a piano, but you can't tuna fish!

What's slimy, tastes of raspberry,
is wobbly and lives in the sea?

A red jellyfish.

How does a jellyfish race start?

Get set.

What did the fish say when he
swam into the wall?

Dam.

What do you call a fish with no eyes?

Fsh.

Where do sharks shop?

The fish market.

What do you call a Russian fish?

A Tsardine.

What kind of fish can you find in a birdcage?

A perch!

Why did the fish cross the sea?

To get to the other tide.

Why did the fish jump out of the water?

Because the seaweed.

What is a little fish's favourite TV show?

Plaice School.

What type of fish is always sleeping?

A kipper.

What do you call a baby whale that
never stops crying?

A little blubber.

Where would you weigh a whale?

At a whale-weigh station?

What does a crab use to call someone?

A shellular phone!

What do you do with a blue whale?

Try to cheer him up!

What do you call a baby whale?

A little squirt.

What shouldn't you do when
you meet a shark?

Go to pieces.

What do you call the autobiography
of a shark?

A fishy story.

Why did the shark take so long
to eat a victim's arm?

*Because the victim's watch made
it time consuming.*

Why was the crab arrested?

Because it kept pinching things.

What lives at the bottom of
the sea with a six gun?

Billy the Squid.

What's an eel's favourite song?

'Slip Sliding Away.'

What kind of sharks never eat women?

Man eating sharks.

What do frogs order in restaurants?

French Flies!

What do you call a frog with no legs?

Unhoppy.

What did the croaking frog
say to her friend?

'I think I've got a person in my throat.'

How did the frog die?

It Kermit-ted suicide.

What do you say to a hitchhiking frog?

'Hop in.'

What is a frog's favourite drink?

Croaka-cola.

What is green and hard?

A frog with a machine gun.

What is Kermit the Frog's middle name?

The.

What's white on the outside,
green on the inside and hops?

A frog sandwich.

Where do musical frogs perform?

At the Sydney Hopera House.

Why can't frogs get life insurance?

Because they are always croaking.

What is green and loud?

A froghorn.

Why did the frog throw away the book?

Because he'd reddit (read it).

Why do frogs like beer?

Because it is made from hops.

What is a tadpole after it is five days old?

Six days old.

What happened to two frogs that caught
the same bug, at the same time?

They got tongue-tied.

Where do tadpoles change into frogs?

The croakroom.

What are teenage giraffes told when
they go on their first date?

No necking.

What did the giraffe say when a car
load of tourists drove past?

'It's terrible the way they're caged up.'

What's the tallest yellow flower in the world?

A giraffodil.

Why do giraffes have long necks?

Because their feet stink.

What do you call a young goat who
visits a psychiatrist?

A mixed-up kid.

Why can't you have a conversation
with a goat?

Because it always butts in.

What is small, brown and squirts jam?

A hamster eating a doughnut.

What do you call a hippo that believes in peace, love and understanding?

A hippie-potamus.

What can go as fast as a race horse?

The jockey!

What has four legs and sees just as well from both ends?

A horse with his eyes closed.

What do you call a pony with a sore throat?

A little horse!

How do you hire a horse?

Put four bricks under his feet.

Where do horses stay in a hotel?

In the bridle suite.

How do you make a slow racehorse fast?

Put it on a diet.

What disease do you have if you're
allergic to horses?

Bronco-itis.

What do you give to a horse
with a sore throat?

Cough stirrup.

Where do sick ponies go?

To the horsepital.

Why do horses only wear shoes?

Because they would look silly with socks on.

Which TV show do horses like best?

Neigh-bours.

What do you call a fly with no wings?

A walk.

What did one firefly say to the
other before he left?

'Bye! I'm glowing now!'

Why did the fly fly?

Because the spider spied her.

What has four wheels and flies?

A wheelie bin.

Why were flies playing football in a saucer?

They were playing for the cup.

Why did the flies run across the top
of the cling wrap box?

Because it read 'Tear along the dotted line.'

What do you call a fly when it retires?

A flew.

What's the difference between
a mosquito and a fly?

Try zipping up a mosquito!

What did the mosquito say when
he saw a camel's hump?

'Gee, did I do that?'

What do you call a mosquito that prefers walking to flying?

An itch-hiker.

What has six legs, bites, buzzes and talks in code?

A morse-quito.

Why did the firefly get bad grades in school?

He wasn't very bright!

How do fireflies start a race?

Ready, steady, glow!

How do you start a flea race?

One, Two, Flea, Go!

What do you call a mad flea?

A looney-tic!

What did one flea say to the other?

'Shall we walk or take the dog?'

What is the biggest ant in the world?

An eleph-ant.

What's even bigger than that?

A gi-ant!

How many ants are needed to
fill an apartment?

Ten-ants.

Where do ants eat?

A restaur-ant.

What is smaller than an ant's mouth?

An ant's dinner.

Why don't anteaters get sick?

Because they're full of ant-ibodies.

Name six things smaller than
an ant's mouth?

Six of its teeth!

What do termites eat for dessert?

Toothpicks.

What is a termite's favourite breakfast?

Oak-meal.

What did the termite say when she saw that her friends had completely eaten a chair?

Wooden you know it!

Why did the termite quit its job?

Because it was boring.

Which insects can tell the time?

Clockroaches.

Which movie character do insects like best?

Bug Lightyear.

Why is the letter 'T' important
to a stick insect?

Because without it, it would be a sick insect.

Why did the lion feel sick after
he'd eaten the priest?

Because it's hard to keep a good man down.

What did the lioness say to the
cub chasing the hunter?

'Stop playing with your food.'

Why did the lion spit out the clown?

Because he tasted funny.

When is a lion not a lion?

When he turns into his den.

What's a lion's favourite food?

Baked beings.

What does a lion brush his mane with?

A catacomb.

How can you get a set of teeth
put in for free?

Tease a lion.

How does a lion say 'hi' to other animals?

'Pleased to eat you!'

What did the lion say to his cubs when
he taught them to hunt?

*'Don't walk across the road until
you see the zebra crossing.'*

What do lions say before they go
out hunting for food?

'Let us prey.'

What should you know if you want
to be a lion tamer?

More than the lion.

What's the difference between a
dark sky and an injured lion.

*One pours with rain, the other
roars with pain.*

Did you hear about the cannibal lioness?

She swallowed her pride.

What did the lion say when a car load
of tourists drove past?

'Meals on wheels.'

What song do lions sing at Christmas?

'Jungle bells.'

What's the difference between
a tiger and a lion?

A tiger has the mane part missing.

Why does a tiger have stripes?

So it won't be spotted.

Why are tigers and sergeants
in the army alike?

They both wear the stripes.

Who went into the tiger's lair
and came out alive?

The tiger.

Why do tigers eat raw meat?

Because they can't cook.

What is striped and bouncy?

A tiger on a pogo stick.

What do tigers wear in bed?

Striped pyjamas!

What do leopards say after lunch?

'That sure hit the spots!'

Why can't a leopard hide?

Because he's always spotted!

What happened to the leopard who took four baths every day?

Within a week he was spotless.

Why did the lizard cross the road?

To see his flat mate.

What does a lizard wear on
special occasions?

A rep-tie.

What has two legs and two tails?

A lizard flipping a coin.

When is it bad luck to see a black cat?

When you're a mouse.

What is grey, has big ears and a trunk?

A mouse going on vacation!

Hickory dickory dock,

Three mice ran up the clock,

The clock struck one,

*But the other two got away
with minor injuries.*

How do you spell "mouse trap"
with three letters?

C A T.

What's the best way to face a timid mouse?

Lie down in front of its mouse hole and cover your nose with cheese spread!

What is a narrow squeak?

A thin mouse!

What do you call a mouse that can pick up a monster?

Sir.

What goes 'dot, dot, dash, squeak'?

Mouse code.

What's the biggest mouse in the world?

A hippopotamouse.

What do you do with a mouse that squeaks?

You oil him.

How do you milk a mouse?

You can't. The bucket won't fit under it.

What do you do if you come across
an unconscious rodent?

Give it mouse to mouse.

Who is emperor of all mice?

Julius Cheeser.

What's small, squeaks, and hangs
out in caves?

Stalagmice.

What is white, fluffy and lives in the jungle?

A meringue-utan!

What happens when a chimpanzee
sprains his ankle?

He gets a monkey wrench.

What's the best way to catch a monkey?

Climb a tree and act like a banana.

What do you call a monkey with
a banana in each ear?

Anything, he can't hear you.

What do patriotic American monkeys wave
on July 4?

Star spangled bananas.

Where do baby monkeys sleep?

In an apricot.

Why did the boy get in trouble for feeding
the monkeys at the zoo?

Because he fed them to the lions.

Where do monkeys cook their dinner?

Under the gorilla.

Which area of the police force
accepts monkeys?

The Special Branch.

Who is the king of the monkeys?

Henry the Ape.

What swings through the trees
and is very dangerous?

A chimpanzee with a machine-gun.

Why do gorillas have big nostrils?

Because they have big fingers.

How can you stop moles digging
up your garden?

Hide the shovel.

What do you call a penguin in the desert?

Lost.

What's black and white and goes
round and round?

A penguin caught in a revolving door.

What's black and white and
rolls down a hill?

A penguin.

What's black and white and laughs?

The penguin who pushed the other one.

What's black and white and
makes a terrible noise?

A penguin playing the bagpipes.

What kind of tie do pigs wear?

A pigsty.

What do you give a pig with a rash?

Oinkment!

Why did the gangster kill his pet pig?

Because it squealed to the police.

Why didn't the piglets listen to their father?

Because he was a boar.

How do you stop a pig from smelling?

Put a peg on his nose.

Where does a pig go to pawn his watch?

A ham hock shop.

A pig walks into a bar and asks for a beer.

Bartender: 'That'll be $5. And by the way, it's nice to see you. We don't get many pigs in here.'

Pig: 'At $5 a beer, I'm not surprised.'

How do pigs get clean.

They go to the hogwash.

What do you call a pig that does karate?

Pork chop.

What do you call a pig who enjoys
jumping from a great height?

A stydiver.

What do you call a tall building
which pigs work in?

A styscraper.

What do you call a pig with no clothes on?

Streaky bacon.

What do you call two pigs who
write letters to each other?

Pen-pals.

What is a pig's favourite ballet?

Swine Lake.

What kind of vehicles do pigs drive?

Pig up trucks.

Where do pigs go for their holidays?

Hamsterdam.

Where do pigs go when they die?

To the sty in the sky.

How do you know that carrots are
good for your eyesight?

Have you ever seen a rabbit wearing glasses?

What did the porcupine say to the cactus?

Are you my mother?

What do you call fourteen rabbits
hopping backwards?

A receding hareline.

What's the best way to catch a rabbit?

*Hide in the bushes and make
a noise like lettuce.*

What do you get when you pour hot
water down a rabbit hole?

Hot cross bunnies.

What did the rabbit give his girlfriend
when they got engaged?

A 24-carrot ring.

How can you tell the difference between
a rabbit and a monster?

*Ever tried getting a monster
into a rabbit hutch?*

Which animals are best at maths?

Rabbits, because they're always multiplying.

How can you tell a rabbit from a gorilla?

A rabbit looks nothing like a gorilla.

How do you stop a rhino from charging?

Take away its credit card!

What do you call a lamb with a machine gun?

Lambo.

'**D**id you know it takes three sheep
to make a sweater?'

'*Hmmm. I didn't even know they could knit.*'

How do sheep get clean?

They have a Baaaaath.

Sheep 1: 'Baa.'

*Sheep 2: 'I knew you were
going to say that.'*

What do you call a sheep in a bikini?

Bra-bra black sheep.

What do you call a shy sheep?

Baaaashful.

What is a sheep's favourite dessert?

A Mars Baaaaa

Where do sheep go on holiday?

Baaaali.

Where do sheep go to get haircuts?

To the Baa Baa shop!

Where do sheep shop?

At Woolworths.

Why did Bo Peep lose her sheep?

She had a crook with her.

Why did the traffic officer book the sheep?

Because it did a ewe turn.

What was the tortoise doing on the freeway?

About three metres an hour.

What type of food can't tortoises eat?

Fast food.

How did the skunk phone his mother?

On a smellular phone.

What did the judge say when he saw
the skunk in the courtroom?

'Odour in the court!'

How many skunks does it take
to stink out a room?

A phew.

What did the skunk say when the
wind changed direction?

'Ahhh, it's all coming back to me now.'

What is the difference between
a wolf and a flea?

*One howls on the prairie, the other
prowls on the hairy.*

What happened when the Big Bad Wolf fell
into Grandma's washing machine?

He became a wash and werewolf.

What did the snail say when he hitched
a ride on the turtle's back?

'Weeeeeeeeeeeeeeeeeeeeeee!!!!'

What is a slug?

A snail with a housing problem.

What do snails apply before
going on a date?

Snail varnish.

What do you do when you see
two snails fighting?

Nothing, you just let them slug it out.

If a snake and an undertaker got married,
what would they put on their towels?

Hiss and Hearse!

Why did the snail paint an S on its car?

So people would say 'Look at that S car go!'

How do you make a snake cry?

Take away its rattle!

What's green and wiggly and goes 'hith'?

A snake with a lisp.

Why do snakes have forked tongues?

Because they can't use chopsticks.

What sort of music is played
most in the jungle?

Snake, rattle and roll.

Did you hear about the acrobatic snake?

He was in Monty Python's Flying Circus.

What do you call a snake that works
for the government?

A civil serpent.

What do you give to a sick snake?

An asp-rin.

What's worse than finding a
worm in your apple?

Finding half a worm!

What is an army of worms called?

An apple corps.

What's the best advice a mother worm
can give to her children?

Sleep late.

What do glow-worms drink?

Light beer.

How do tell which end of
a worm is the head?

*Tickle him in the middle and
watch where he smiles.*

What is a snake's favourite opera?

'Wrigoletto.'

What is the favourite class for snakes?

Hiss-tory.

Why can't you play a practical
joke on snakes?

Because they don't have a leg to pull.

Why did the viper vipe her nose?

Because the adder ad 'er 'ankerchief.

What did the boa constrictor say to its victim?

'I've got a crush on you.'

What's black and white and hides in caves?

A zebra who owes money.

What's black and white and eats like a horse?

A zebra.

What's striped and goes round and round?

A zebra on a merry-go-round.

What is black and white and red all over?

A sunburned zebra.

What do you call two spiders
who just got married?

Newlywebs!

How do you know when a spider is cool?

It has its own website.

What's the difference between
a unicorn and a lettuce?

*One is a funny beast and the
other a bunny feast.*

What do you get when you cross a cocker
spaniel with a rooster and a **poodle?**

Cockerpoodledoo.

What do you get when you cross
a chicken and a caterpillar?

Drumsticks for everyone!

What do you get when you cross a
mountain lion and a parrot?

*I don't know, but when it talks,
you had better listen!*

What do you get when you cross
a high chair and a bird?

A stool pigeon.

What do you get when you cross
a duck with a rooster?

*A bird that wakes you up
at the quack of dawn!*

What do you get when you
cross a rooster with a steer?

A cock and bull story.

'My parrot lays square eggs.'

'That's amazing! Can it talk as well?'

'Yes, but only one word.'

'What's that?'

'Ouch!'

What do get if you cross a
centipede with a parrot?

A walkie-talkie.

What do you get when you cross
a skunk with a bear?

Winnie the Poo.

What do you get when you cross
a duck with a firework?

A fire-quacker.

What do you get when you cross
a chicken with a yo-yo?

A bird that lays the same egg three times!

What do you get when you cross
an elephant with peanut butter?

*Either an elephant that sticks to
the roof of your mouth or peanut
butter that never forgets.*

What do you get when you cross
an alligator with a camera?

A snapshot.

What do get when you cross
a dog and a cat?

An animal that chases itself.

What do you get when you cross
a giraffe with an echidna?

A ten metre toothbrush.

What do you get when you cross a
hunting dog with a journalist?

A news hound.

What do you get when you cross a
leopard with a watchdog?

A terrified postman.

What do you get when you cross a
bottle of water with an electric eel?

A bit of a shock!

What do you get when you cross
an eel with a shopper?

A crazy customer.

What do you get when you cross
an elephant with a sparrow?

Broken telephone poles everywhere.

What do you get when you cross
a parrot with a shark?

A bird that will talk your ear off!

What do you get when you cross an
electric eel with a sponge?

Shock absorbers.

What do you get when you cross
a frog with a small dog?

A croaker spaniel.

What do you get when you cross a
parrot with a woodpecker?

A bird that talks in Morse code.

What do you get when you cross
a corgi with a clock?

A watchdog.

What do you get when you cross
a dog with a vegetable?

A jack brussell.

What do you get when you cross
a monkey with a flower?

A chimp-pansy.

What do you get when you cross a
baby rabbit with a vegetable?

A bunion.

What do you get when you cross
a cat with a lemon?

A sour puss!

What do you get when you cross a
black bird with a madman?

A raven lunatic.

What do you get when you cross
a bear with a cow?

Winnie the Moo.

What do you get when you cross a
chicken with a cement mixer?

A bricklayer.

What do you get when you cross a
Chinese leader with a cat?

Miaow Tse Tung.

What do you get when you cross a
cow with a clairvoyant?

A message from the udder side.

What do you get when you cross
a cow with a duck?

Cream quackers.

What do you get when you cross a chicken
with a mild-mannered reporter?

Cluck Kent.

What do you get when you cross
a cow with a whale?

Mooby dick.

What do you get when you cross a
frog with a native American?

A toadempole.

What do you get when you cross
a flea with a comedian?

A nitwit.

What do you get when you cross a flower
with a big cat who wears a cravat?

A dandelion.

What do you get when you cross a hare
with a walking stick?

A hurry-cane (hurricane).

What do you get when you cross
a hippopotamus with someone
who is always sick?

A hippochondriac.

What do you get when you cross a jungle
animal with an accountant?

A wild bore.

What do you get when you cross a
kookaburra with a jug of gravy?

A laughing stock.

What do you get when you cross a
master criminal with a fish?

The Codfather.

What do you get when you cross
a tiger with a sheep?

A striped sweater.

What do you get when you cross
a tiger with a snowman?

Frostbite.

What do you get when you cross
a kangaroo with a skyscraper?

A high jumper.

What do you get when you cross
a mouse and a deer?

Mickey Moose.

What do you get when you cross
a mouse with an orange?

A pipsqueak.

What do you get when you cross
a parrot with a soldier?

A parrot trooper.

What do you get when you cross a seagull
with a pair of wheels?

A bi-seagull.

What do you get when you cross
a sheep with a radiator?

Central bleating.

What do you get when you cross a skunk
with a table tennis ball?

Ping pong.

What do you get when you cross
Bambi with a ghost?

Bamboo.

What do you get when you cross a tiger
with a kangaroo?

A striped jumper.

What do you get when you cross a
snake with some Lego?

A boa constructor.

What do you get when you cross
a skunk with an owl?

A bird who stinks but doesn't give a hoot.

What do you get when you cross a
watch with a parrot?

Politicks.

What do you get when you cross a
wedding with a cliff?

A marriage that is on the rocks.

What do you get when you cross a
witch and a skunk?

An ugly smell.

What do you get when you cross an elephant
with a bottle of rum?

Trunk and disorderly.

What do you get when you cross a
pig with a zebra?

Striped sausages.

What do you get when you cross
an elephant with a cake?

Crumbs.

What do you get when you cross
a hyena with an Oxo cube?

*An animal which makes a
laughing stock of itself.*

What do you get when you cross
an elephant with a rhino?

Elifino.

What do you get if you cross a witch's
cat with Father Christmas?

Santa Claws.

What do you get if you cross a
homing pigeon with a parrot?

*A bird that asks for directions
when it gets lost.*